DIAMOND PAINTING 911

DMC Color Chart Book for Diamond Painting

The Complete Table (2019 DMC Color Card)

2nd Edition

http://www.diamondpainting911.com
https://www.facebook.com/diamondpainting911

ISBN-13: 978-1-947880-07-8

DIAMOND PAINTING 911

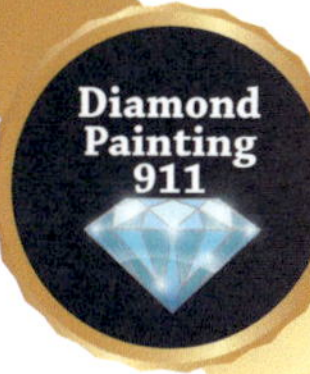

Today I'm going to show you the 2nd edition of our very effective DMC Color Chart Book for 2019.

In fact, I recently used this exact book to assign DMC codes to a batch of unlabelled drills.

You might already know that DMC uses over 450 colors …

But what are they?

Some are clearly different.

Some are very similar.

They can be difficult to distinguish from one another.

But they're all here.

Well, you're in for a treat! Because I've put together a complete list in this book!

I recently updated this book to this second edition, providing you with 4 different charts:

- Chart #1: DA VINCI Chart
- Chart #2: WARHOL Chart
- Chart #3: VAN GOGH Chart
- Chart #4: PICASSO Chart

And the best thing is that every chart has a special column to glue drills next to each color.

DIAMOND PAINTING 911

These charts can be used for

#1: Drills without DMC Number

Have you ever had bags of drills with no DMC numbers?
Multiple bags of colors can be a chore to label. The VAN GOGH
chart can help you with this.

#2: Drills with unknown DMC number

Do you have drills that you do not know the number for?
The PICASSO chart can help you discover these in record time!

#3: Diamond painting kit without drills

If your kit arrives without drills, you can complete the kit from
your own reserves using the legend and the DA VINCI chart to
give you the exact color. You can also use the WARHOL chart
here, as it condenses all charts into one, allowing for better color
palette visualisation.

#4: Diamond painting kit with substituted drills

Recently I've received some DPs where the seller substituted the
drills. I was keen to see how close the shades were and
decide whether I needed to hunt down the correct DMC shade.
You can use the charts as a reference guide to ensure that the
substitutions are accurate, before contacting the seller or pur-
chasing replacement drills.

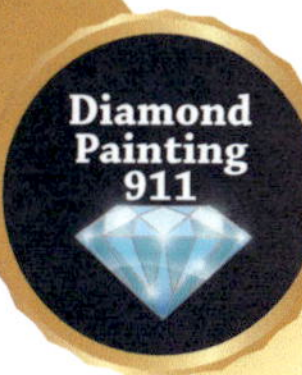

#5: Bad Shade Drills

If you do not like a shade in a DP and want to find substitute drills to purchase separately. The charts can help you with that.

#6: Drills with same DMC codes between sellers

Not all drills are created equal! Drills are often different, despite having the same DMC codes. You can use our charts to help you standardise your supplies.

#7: Aesthetically pleasing chart

The charts are also beautiful. A visually stunning spectrum of colors that brighten any workspace.

There you have it: The 2019 DMC Color Chart Book. Which tip from this book you want to try the chart for? Why not start now and life hack your DP work today!

DMC	Color	Drill	Name	DMC	Color	Drill	Name
Ecru			Ecru/off-white	321			Red
Blanc			White	322			Baby Blue
B5200			Snow White	326			Rose - VY DK
White			White	327			Violet
150			Red - BRIGHT	333			Blue Violet - VY DK
151			Pink	334			Baby Blue - MED
152			Tawny - DK	335			Rose
153			Lilac	336			Blue
154			Red - VY DK	340			Blue Violet - MED
155			Forget-me-not Blue	341			Blue Violet - LT
156			Blue - MED	347			Salmon - VY DK
157			Blue - LT	349			Coral - DK
158			Blue - DK	350			Coral - MED
159			Petrol Blue - LT	351			Coral
160			Petrol Blue - MED	352			Coral - LT
161			Petrol Blue - DK	353			Peach
162			Baby Blue - LT	355			Terra Cotta - DK
163			Green	356			Terra Cotta - MED
164			Green - LT	367			Pistachio Green - DK
165			Green - BRIGHT	368			Pistachio Green - LT
166			Lime Green	369			Pistachio Green - VY LT
167			Khaki Brown	370			Mustard - MED
168			Silver Gray	371			Mustard
169			Pewter Gray	372			Mustard - LT
208			Lavender - VY DK	400			Mahogany - DK
209			Lavender - DK	402			Mahogany - VY LT
210			Lavender - MED	407			Desert Sand - DK
211			Lavender - LT	413			Pewter Gray - DK
221			Shell Pink - VY DK	414			Steel Gray - DK
223			Shell Pink - LT	415			Pearl Gray
224			Shell Pink - VY LT	420			Hazelnut Brown - DK
225			Shell Pink - ULT VY LT	422			Hazelnut Brown - LT
300			Mahogany - VY DK	433			Brown - MED
301			Mahogany - MED	434			Brown - LT
304			Red - MED	435			Brown - VY LT
307			Lemon	436			Tan
309			Rose - DK	437			Tan - LT
310			Black	444			Lemon - DK
311			Blue - MED	445			Lemon - LT
312			Baby Blue - VY DK	451			Sholl Gray - DK
315			Antique Mauve - MED DK	452			Shell Gray - MED
316			Antique Mauve - MED	453			Shell Gray - LT
317			Pewter Gray	469			Avocado Green
318			Steel Gray - LT	470			Avocado Green - LT
319			Pistachio Green - VY DK	471			Avocado Green - VY LT
320			Pistachio Green - MED	472			Avocado Green - ULT LT

DMC	Color	Drill	Name	DMC	Color	Drill	Name
498			Red - DK	647			Beaver Gray - MED
500			Blue Green - VY DK	648			Beaver Gray - LT
501			Blue Green - DK	666			Red - BRIGHT
502			Blue Green	676			Old Gold - LT
503			Blue Green - MED	677			Old Gold - VY LT
504			Blue Green - VY LT	680			Old Gold - DK
505			Grass Green - DK	699			Green
517			Wedgewood - DK	700			Green - BRIGHT
518			Wedgewood - LT	701			Green - LT
519			Sky Blue	702			Kelly Green
520			Fern Green - DK	703			Chartreuse
522			Fern Green	704			Chartreuse - BRIGHT
523			Fern Green - LT	712			Cream
524			Fern Green - VY LT	718			Plum
535			Ash Gray - VY LT	720			Orange Spice - DK
543			Beige Brown - ULT VY LT	721			Orange Spice - MED
550			Violet - VY DK	722			Orange Spice - LT
552			Violet - MED	725			Topaz
553			Violet	726			Topaz - LT
554			Violet - LT	727			Topaz - VY LT
561			Jade - VY DK	728			Golden Yellow
562			Jade - MED	729			Old Gold - MED
563			Jade - LT	730			Olive Green - VY DK
564			Jade - VY LT	731			Ollve Green - DK
580			Moss Green - DK	732			Olive Green
581			Moss Green	733			Olive Green - MED
597			Turquoise	734			Olive Green - LT
598			Turquoise - LT	738			Tan - VY LT
600			Cranberry - VY DK	739			Tan - ULT VY LT
601			Cranberry - DK	740			Tangerine
602			Cranberry - MED	741			Tangerine - MED
603			Cranberry	742			Tangerine - LT
604			Cranberry - LT	743			Yellow - MED
605			Cranberry - VY LT	744			Yellow - PALE
606			Orange-red - BRIGHT	745			Yellow - LT PALE
608			Orange - BRIGHT	746			Off White
610			Drab Brown - DK	747			Sky Blue - VY LT
611			Drab Brown	754			Peach - LT
612			Drab Brown - LT	758			Terra Cotta - VY LT
613			Drab Drown - VY LT	760			Salmon
632			Desert Sand - ULT VY DK	761			Salmon - LT
640			Beige Gray - VY DK	762			Pearl Gray - VY LT
642			Beige Gray - DK	772			Yellow Green - VY LT
644			Beige Gray - MED	775			Baby Blue - VY LT
645			Beaver Gray - VY DK	776			Pink - MED
646			Beaver Gray - DK	777			Red - DEEP

DMC	Color	Drill	Name	DMC	Color	Drill	Name
778			Antique Mauve - VY LT	844			Beaver Gray - ULT DK
779			Brown	868			Hazel Nut Brown
780			Topaz - ULT VY DK	869			Hazelnut Brown - VY DK
781			Topaz - VY DK	890			Pistachio Green - ULT DK
782			Topaz - DK	891			Carnation - DK
783			Topaz - MED	892			Carnation - MED
791			Cornflower Blue - VY DK	893			Carnation - LT
792			Cornflower Blue - DK	894			Carnation - VY LT
793			Cornflower Blue - MED	895			Hunter Green - VY DK
794			Cornflower Blue - LT	898			Coffee Brown - VY DK
796			Royal Blue - DK	899			Rose - MED
797			Royal Blue	900			Burnt Orange - DK
798			Delft Blue - DK	902			Garnet - VY DK
799			Delft Blue - MED	904			Parrot Green - VY DK
800			Delft Blue - PALE	905			Parrot Green - DK
801			Coffee Brown - DK	906			Parrot Green - MED
803			Blue - DEEP	907			Parrot Green - LT
806			Peacock Blue - DK	909			Emerald Green - VY DK
807			Peacock Blue	910			Emerald Green - DK
809			Delft Blue	911			Emerald Green - MED
813			Blue - LT	912			Emerald Green - LT
814			Garnet - DK	913			Nile Green - MED
815			Garnet - MED	915			Plum - DK
816			Garnet	917			Plum - MED
817			Coral Red - VY DK	918			Red Copper - DK
818			Baby Pink	919			Red Copper
819			Baby Pink - LT	920			Copper - MED
820			Royal Blue - VY DK	921			Copper
822			Beige Gray - LT	922			Copper - LT
823			Blue - DK	924			Gray Green - VY DK
824			Blue - VY DK	926			Gray Green - MED
825			Blue - DK	927			Gray Green - LT
826			Blue - MED	928			Gray Green - VY LT
827			Blue - VY LT	930			Antique Blue - DK
828			Blue - ULT VY LT	931			Antique Blue - MED
829			Golden Olive - VY DK	932			Antique Blue - LT
830			Golden Olive - DK	934			Avocado Green - BLACK
831			Golden Olive - MED	935			Avocado Green - DK
832			Golden Olive	936			Avocado Green - VY DK
833			Golden Olive - LT	937			Avocado Green - MED
834			Golden Olive - VY LT	938			Coffee Brown - ULT DK
838			Beige Brown - VY DK	939			Blue - VY DK
839			Beige Brown - DK	943			Aquamarine - MED
840			Beige Brown - MED	945			Tawny
841			Beige Brown - LT	946			Burnt Orange - MED
842			Beige Brown - VY LT	947			Burnt Orange

DMC	Color	Drill	Name
948			Peach - VY LT
950			Desert Sand - LT
951			Tawny - LT
954			Nile Green
955			Nile Green - LT
956			Geranium
957			Geranium - PALE
958			Seagreen - DK
959			Seagreen - MED
961			Dusty Rose - DK
962			Dusty Rose - MED
963			Dusty Rose - ULT VY LT
964			Seagreen - LT
966			Baby Green - MED
967			Peach - LT
970			Pumpkin - LT
971			Pumpkin
972			Canary - DEEP
973			Canary - BRIGHT
975			Golden Brown - DK
976			Golden Brown - MED
977			Golden Brown - LT
986			Forest Green - VY DK
987			Forest Green - DK
988			Forest Green - MED
989			Forest Green
991			Aquamarine - DK
992			Aquamarine - LT
993			Aquamarine - VY LT
995			Electric Blue - DK
996			Electric Blue - MED
3011			Khaki Green - DK
3012			Khaki Green - MED
3013			Khaki Green - LT
3021			Brown Gray - VY DK
3022			Brown Gray - MED
3023			Brown Gray - LT
3024			Brown Gray - VY LT
3031			Mocha Brown - VY DK
3032			Mocha Brown - MED
3033			Mocha Brown - VY LT
3041			Antique Violet - MED
3042			Antique Violet - LT
3045			Yellow Beige - DK
3046			Yellow Beige - MED

DMC	Color	Drill	Name
3047			Yellow Beige - LT
3051			Green Gray - DK
3052			Green Gray - MED
3053			Green Gray
3064			Desert Sand
3072			Beaver Gray - VY LT
3078			Golden Yellow - VY LT
3325			Baby Blue - LT
3326			Rose - LT
3328			Salmon - DK
3340			Apricot - MED
3341			Apricot
3345			Hunter Green - DK
3346			Hunter Green
3347			Yellow Green - MED
3348			Yellow Green - LT
3350			Dusty Rose - ULT DK
3354			Dusty Rose - LT
3362			Pine Green - DK
3363			Pine Green - MED
3364			Pine Green
3371			Black Brown
3607			Plum - LT
3608			Plum - VY LT
3609			Plum - ULT LT
3685			Mauve - VY DK
3687			Mauve
3688			Mauve - MED
3689			Mauve - LT
3705			Melon - DK
3706			Melon - MED
3708			Melon - LT
3712			Salmon - MED
3713			Salmon - VY LT
3716			Dusty Rose - VY LT
3721			Shell Pink - DK
3722			Shell Pink - MED
3726			Antique Mauve - DK
3727			Antique Mauve - LT
3731			Dusty Rose - VY DK
3733			Dusty Rose
3740			Antique Violet - DK
3743			Antique Violet - VY LT
3746			Blue Violet - DK
3747			Blue Violet - VY LT

DMC	Color	Drill	Name
3750			Antique Blue - VY DK
3752			Antique Blue - VY LT
3753			Antique Blue - ULT VY LT
3755			Baby Blue (?)
3756			Baby Blue
3760			Wedgewood - MED
3761			Sky Blue - LT
3765			Peacock Blue - VY DK
3766			Peacock Blue - LT
3768			Gray Green - DK
3770			Tawny - VY LT
3771			Peach - DK
3772			Desert Sand - VY DK
3773			Desert Sand - MED
3774			Desert Sand - VY LT
3776			Mahogany - LT
3777			Terra Cotta - VY DK
3778			Terra Cotta - LT
3779			Terra Cotta - ULT VY LT
3781			Mocha Brown - DK
3782			Mocha Brown - LT
3787			Brown Gray - DK
3790			Beige Gray - ULT DK
3799			Pewter Gray - VY DK
3801			Melon - VY DK
3802			Antique Mauve - VY DK
3803			Mauve - DK
3804			Cyclamen Pink - DK
3805			Cyclamen Pink
3806			Cyclamen Pink - LT
3807			Cornflower Blue
3808			Turquoise - ULT VY DK
3809			Turquoise - VY DK
3810			Turquoise - DK
3811			Turquoise - VY LT
3812			Seagreen - VY DK
3813			Blue Green - LT
3814			Aquamarine
3815			Celadon Green - DK
3816			Celadon Green
3817			Celadon Green - LT
3818			Emerald Green - ULT VY DK
3819			Moss Green - LT
3820			Straw - DK
3821			Straw

DMC	Color	Drill	Name
3822			Straw - LT
3823			Yellow - ULT PALE
3824			Apricot - LT
3825			Pumpkin - PALE
3826			Golden Brown
3827			Golden Brown - PALE
3828			Hazelnut Brown
3829			Old Gold - VY DK
3830			Terra Cotta
3831			Raspberry - DK
3832			Raspberry - MED
3833			Raspberry - LT
3834			Grape - DK
3835			Grape - MED
3836			Grape - LT
3837			Lavender - ULT DK
3838			Lavender Blue - DK
3839			Lavender Blue - MED
3840			Lavender Blue - LT
3841			Baby Blue - PALE
3842			Wedgewood - DK
3843			Electric Blue
3844			Bright Turquoise - DK
3845			Bright Turquoise - MED
3846			Bright Turquoise - LT
3847			Teal Green - DK
3848			Teal Green - MED
3849			Teal Green - LT
3850			Bright Green - DK
3851			Bright Green - LT
3852			Straw - VY DK
3853			Autumn Gold - DK
3854			Autumn Gold - MED
3855			Autumn Gold - LT
3856			Mahogany - ULT VY LT
3857			Rosewood - DK
3858			Rosewood - MED
3859			Rosewood - LT
3860			Cocoa
3861			Cocoa - LT
3862			Mocha Beige - DK
3863			Mocha Beige - MED
3864			Mocha Beige - LT
3865			Winter White
3866			Mocha Brown - ULT VY LT

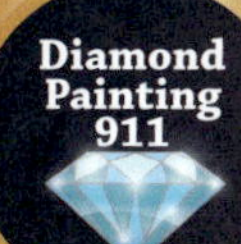

DMC	Color	Drill	DMC	Color	Drill	DMC	Color	Drill	DMC	Color	Drill	DMC	Color	Drill	DMC	Color	Drill
Ecru			420			720			841			993			3774		
Blanc			422			721			842			995			3776		
B5200			433			722			844			996			3777		
White			434			725			868			3011			3778		
150			435			726			869			3012			3779		
151			436			727			890			3013			3781		
152			437			728			891			3021			3782		
153			444			729			892			3022			3787		
154			445			730			893			3023			3790		
155			451			731			894			3024			3799		
156			452			732			895			3031			3801		
157			453			733			898			3032			3802		
158			469			734			899			3033			3803		
159			470			738			900			3041			3804		
160			471			739			902			3042			3805		
161			472			740			904			3045			3806		
162			498			741			905			3046			3807		
163			500			742			906			3047			3808		
164			501			743			907			3051			3809		
165			502			744			909			3052			3810		
166			503			745			910			3053			3811		
167			504			746			911			3064			3812		
168			505			747			912			3072			3813		
169			517			754			913			3078			3814		
208			518			758			915			3325			3815		
209			519			760			917			3326			3816		
210			520			761			918			3328			3817		
211			522			762			919			3340			3818		
221			523			772			920			3341			3819		
223			524			775			921			3345			3820		
224			535			776			922			3346			3821		
225			543			777			924			3347			3822		
300			550			778			926			3348			3823		
301			552			779			927			3350			3824		
304			553			780			928			3354			3825		
307			554			781			930			3362			3826		
309			561			782			931			3363			3827		
310			562			783			932			3364			3828		
311			563			791			934			3371			3829		
312			564			792			935			3607			3830		
315			580			793			936			3608			3831		
316			581			794			937			3609			3832		
317			597			796			938			3685			3833		
318			598			797			939			3687			3834		
319			600			798			943			3688			3835		
320			601			799			945			3689			3836		
321			602			800			946			3705			3837		
322			603			801			947			3706			3838		
326			604			803			948			3708			3839		
327			605			806			950			3712			3840		
333			606			807			951			3713			3841		
334			608			809			954			3716			3842		
335			610			813			955			3721			3843		
336			611			814			956			3722			3844		
340			612			815			957			3726			3845		
341			613			816			958			3727			3846		
347			632			817			959			3731			3847		
349			640			818			961			3733			3848		
350			642			819			962			3740			3849		
351			644			820			963			3743			3850		
352			645			822			964			3746			3851		
353			646			823			966			3747			3852		
355			647			824			907			3750			3853		
356			648			825			970			3752			3854		
367			666			826			971			3753			3855		
368			676			827			972			3755			3856		
369			677			828			973			3756			3857		
370			680			829			975			3760			3858		
371			699			830			976			3761			3859		
372			700			831			977			3765			3860		
400			701			832			986			3766			3861		
402			702			833			987			3768			3862		
407			703			834			988			3770			3863		
413			704			838			989			3771			3864		
414			712			839			991			3772			3865		
415			718			840			992			3773			3866		

DMC	Color	Drill	Name	DMC	Color	Drill	Name
3713			Salmon - VY LT	152			Tawny - DK
761			Salmon - LT	3733			Dusty Rose
760			Salmon	3731			Dusty Rose - VY DK
3712			Salmon - MED	3350			Dusty Rose - ULT DK
3328			Salmon - DK	3689			Mauve - LT
347			Salmon - VY DK	3688			Mauve - MED
353			Peach	3687			Mauve
352			Coral - LT	3803			Mauve - DK
351			Coral	3685			Mauve - VY DK
350			Coral - MED	225			Shell Pink - ULT VY LT
349			Coral - DK	224			Shell Pink - VY LT
817			Coral Red - VY DK	223			Shell Pink - LT
3708			Melon - LT	3722			Shell Pink - MED
3706			Melon - MED	3721			Shell Pink - DK
3705			Melon - DK	221			Shell Pink - VY DK
3801			Melon - VY DK	778			Antique Mauve - VY LT
666			Red - BRIGHT	3727			Antique Mauve - LT
321			Red	316			Antique Mauve - MED
777			Red - DEEP	3726			Antique Mauve - DK
304			Red - MED	315			Antique Mauve - MED DK
498			Red - DK	3802			Antique Mauve - VY DK
816			Garnet	902			Garnet - VY DK
815			Garnet - MED	3042			Antique Violet - LT
814			Garnet - DK	3041			Antique Violet - MED
894			Carnation - VY LT	3740			Antique Violet - DK
893			Carnation - LT	154			Red - VY DK
892			Carnation - MED	3836			Grape - LT
891			Carnation - DK	3835			Grape - MED
957			Geranium - PALE	3834			Grape - DK
956			Geranium	3806			Cyclamen Pink - LT
963			Dusty Rose - ULT VY LT	3805			Cyclamen Pink
3716			Dusty Rose - VY LT	3804			Cyclamen Pink - DK
962			Dusty Rose - MED	151			Pink
961			Dusty Rose - DK	605			Cranberry - VY LT
3833			Raspberry - LT	604			Cranberry - LT
3832			Raspberry - MED	603			Cranberry
3831			Raspberry - DK	602			Cranberry - MED
819			Baby Pink - LT	601			Cranberry - DK
818			Baby Pink	150			Red - BRIGHT
776			Pink - MED	600			Cranberry - VY DK
3326			Rose - LT	3609			Plum - ULT LT
899			Rose - MED	3608			Plum - VY LT
335			Rose	3607			Plum - LT
309			Rose - DK	718			Plum
326			Rose - VY DK	917			Plum - MED
3354			Dusty Rose - LT	915			Plum - DK

DMC	Color	Drill	Name
554			Violet - LT
553			Violet
552			Violet - MED
550			Violet - VY DK
153			Lilac
211			Lavender - LT
210			Lavender - MED
209			Lavender - DK
208			Lavender - VY DK
3837			Lavender - ULT DK
327			Violet
3747			Blue Violet - VY LT
341			Blue Violet - LT
156			Blue - MED
155			Forget-me-not Blue
340			Blue Violet - MED
3746			Blue Violet - DK
333			Blue Violet - VY DK
794			Cornflower Blue - LT
793			Cornflower Blue - MED
792			Cornflower Blue - DK
791			Cornflower Blue - VY DK
158			Blue - DK
803			Blue - DEEP
3807			Cornflower Blue
3840			Lavender Blue - LT
3839			Lavender Blue - MED
3838			Lavender Blue - DK
800			Delft Blue - PALE
809			Delft Blue
799			Delft Blue - MED
798			Delft Blue - DK
797			Royal Blue
796			Royal Blue - DK
820			Royal Blue - VY DK
828			Blue - ULT VY LT
827			Blue - VY LT
813			Blue - LT
826			Blue - MED
825			Blue - DK
824			Blue - VY DK
3756			Baby Blue
775			Baby Blue - VY LT
3841			Baby Blue - PALE
3325			Baby Blue - LT
3755			Baby Blue (?)

DMC	Color	Drill	Name
334			Baby Blue - MED
322			Baby Blue
312			Baby Blue - VY DK
311			Blue - MED
336			Blue
823			Blue - DK
939			Blue - VY DK
505			Grass Green - DK
3753			Antique Blue - ULT VY LT
3752			Antique Blue - VY LT
932			Antique Blue - LT
931			Antique Blue - MED
930			Antique Blue - DK
3750			Antique Blue - VY DK
157			Blue - LT
159			Petrol Blue - LT
160			Petrol Blue - MED
161			Petrol Blue - DK
996			Electric Blue - MED
3843			Electric Blue
995			Electric Blue - DK
3846			Bright Turquoise - LT
3845			Bright Turquoise - MED
3844			Bright Turquoise - DK
3761			Sky Blue - LT
519			Sky Blue
518			Wedgewood - LT
3760			Wedgewood - MED
517			Wedgewood - DK
3842			Wedgewood - DK
162			Baby Blue - LT
747			Sky Blue - VY LT
3765			Peacock Blue - VY DK
3766			Peacock Blue - LT
807			Peacock Blue
806			Peacock Blue - DK
3811			Turquoise - VY LT
598			Turquoise - LT
597			Turquoise
3810			Turquoise - DK
3809			Turquoise - VY DK
3808			Turquoise - ULT VY DK
3849			Teal Green - LT
3848			Teal Green - MED
3847			Teal Green - DK
964			Seagreen - LT

DMC	Color	Drill	Name
959			Seagreen - MED
958			Seagreen - DK
3812			Seagreen - VY DK
3851			Bright Green - LT
943			Aquamarine - MED
3850			Bright Green - DK
993			Aquamarine - VY LT
992			Aquamarine - LT
3814			Aquamarine
991			Aquamarine - DK
564			Jade - VY LT
563			Jade - LT
562			Jade - MED
561			Jade - VY DK
3817			Celadon Green - LT
3816			Celadon Green
3815			Celadon Green - DK
504			Blue Green - VY LT
3813			Blue Green - LT
503			Blue Green - MED
502			Blue Green
501			Blue Green - DK
500			Blue Green - VY DK
928			Gray Green - VY LT
927			Gray Green - LT
168			Silver Gray
169			Pewter Gray
926			Gray Green - MED
3768			Gray Green - DK
924			Gray Green - VY DK
955			Nile Green - LT
954			Nile Green
913			Nile Green - MED
912			Emerald Green - LT
911			Emerald Green - MED
910			Emerald Green - DK
909			Emerald Green - VY DK
3818			Emerald Green - ULT VY DK
163			Green
164			Green - LT
966			Baby Green - MED
369			Pistachio Green - VY LT
368			Pistachio Green - LT
320			Pistachio Green - MED
367			Pistachio Green - DK
319			Pistachio Green - VY DK

DMC	Color	Drill	Name
890			Pistachio Green - ULT DK
989			Forest Green
988			Forest Green - MED
987			Forest Green - DK
986			Forest Green - VY DK
772			Yellow Green - VY LT
3348			Yellow Green - LT
3347			Yellow Green - MED
3346			Hunter Green
3345			Hunter Green - DK
895			Hunter Green - VY DK
704			Chartreuse - BRIGHT
703			Chartreuse
702			Kelly Green
701			Green - LT
700			Green - BRIGHT
699			Green
907			Parrot Green - LT
906			Parrot Green - MED
905			Parrot Green - DK
904			Parrot Green - VY DK
472			Avocado Green - ULT LT
471			Avocado Green - VY LT
470			Avocado Green - LT
469			Avocado Green
937			Avocado Green - MED
936			Avocado Green - VY DK
935			Avocado Green - DK
934			Avocado Green - BLACK
3053			Green Gray
3052			Green Gray - MED
3051			Green Gray - DK
524			Fern Green - VY LT
523			Fern Green - LT
522			Fern Green
520			Fern Green - DK
3364			Pine Green
3363			Pine Green - MED
3362			Pine Green - DK
165			Green - BRIGHT
3819			Moss Green - LT
166			Lime Green
581			Moss Green
580			Moss Green - DK
734			Olive Green - LT
733			Olive Green - MED

DMC	Color	Drill	Name
732			Olive Green
731			Olive Green - DK
730			Olive Green - VY DK
3013			Khaki Green - LT
3012			Khaki Green - MED
3011			Khaki Green - DK
372			Mustard - LT
371			Mustard
370			Mustard - MED
834			Golden Olive - VY LT
833			Golden Olive - LT
832			Golden Olive
831			Golden Olive - MED
167			Khaki Brown
830			Golden Olive - DK
829			Golden Olive - VY DK
613			Drab Brown - VY LT
612			Drab Brown - LT
611			Drab Brown
610			Drab Brown - DK
3047			Yellow Beige - LT
3046			Yellow Beige - MED
3045			Yellow Beige - DK
677			Old Gold - VY LT
422			Hazelnut Brown - LT
3828			Hazelnut Brown
869			Hazelnut Brown - VY DK
420			Hazelnut Brown - DK
783			Topaz - MED
782			Topaz - DK
781			Topaz - VY DK
780			Topaz - ULT VY DK
746			Off White
676			Old Gold - LT
729			Old Gold - MED
680			Old Gold - DK
3829			Old Gold - VY DK
3822			Straw - LT
3821			Straw
3820			Straw - DK
3852			Straw - VY DK
445			Lemon - LT
307			Lemon
444			Lemon - DK
3078			Golden Yellow - VY LT

DMC	Color	Drill	Name
727			Topaz - VY LT
726			Topaz - LT
725			Topaz
3823			Yellow - ULT PALE
745			Yellow - LT PALE
744			Yellow - PALE
743			Yellow - MED
728			Golden Yellow
742			Tangerine - LT
741			Tangerine - MED
740			Tangerine
973			Canary - BRIGHT
972			Canary - DEEP
971			Pumpkin
970			Pumpkin - LT
947			Burnt Orange
946			Burnt Orange - MED
900			Burnt Orange - DK
608			Orange - BRIGHT
606			Orange-red - BRIGHT
3824			Apricot - LT
3341			Apricot
3340			Apricot - MED
3825			Pumpkin - PALE
722			Orange Spice - LT
721			Orange Spice - MED
720			Orange Spice - DK
922			Copper - LT
921			Copper
920			Copper - MED
919			Red Copper
918			Red Copper - DK
3770			Tawny - VY LT
951			Tawny - LT
945			Tawny
3856			Mahogany - ULT VY LT
402			Mahogany - VY LT
3776			Mahogany - LT
301			Mahogany - MED
400			Mahogany - DK
300			Mahogany - VY DK
3855			Autumn Gold - LT
3854			Autumn Gold - MED
3853			Autumn Gold - DK
3827			Golden Brown - PALE

DMC	Color	Drill	Name
977			Golden Brown - LT
976			Golden Brown - MED
3826			Golden Brown
975			Golden Brown - DK
948			Peach - VY LT
754			Peach - LT
758			Terra Cotta - VY LT
3778			Terra Cotta - LT
356			Terra Cotta - MED
3830			Terra Cotta
355			Terra Cotta - DK
3777			Terra Cotta - VY DK
967			Peach - LT
3779			Terra Cotta - ULT VY LT
3859			Rosewood - LT
3858			Rosewood - MED
3857			Rosewood - DK
3774			Desert Sand - VY LT
950			Desert Sand - LT
3771			Peach - DK
3773			Desert Sand - MED
3064			Desert Sand
407			Desert Sand - DK
3772			Desert Sand - VY DK
632			Desert Sand - ULT VY DK
3743			Antique Violet - VY LT
453			Shell Gray - LT
452			Shell Gray - MED
451			Shell Gray - DK
3861			Cocoa - LT
3860			Cocoa
712			Cream
739			Tan - ULT VY LT
738			Tan - VY LT
437			Tan - LT
436			Tan
435			Brown - VY LT
868			Hazel Nut Brown
434			Brown - LT
433			Brown - MED
801			Coffee Brown - DK
898			Coffee Brown - VY DK
938			Coffee Brown - ULT DK
3371			Black Brown
543			Beige Brown - ULT VY LT

DMC	Color	Drill	Name
3864			Mocha Beige - LT
3863			Mocha Beige - MED
3862			Mocha Beige - DK
842			Beige Brown - VY LT
841			Beige Brown - LT
840			Beige Brown - MED
839			Beige Brown - DK
779			Brown
838			Beige Brown - VY DK
3790			Beige Gray - ULT DK
3781			Mocha Brown - DK
3031			Mocha Brown - VY DK
White			White
B5200			Snow White
Blanc			White
3865			Winter White
Ecru			Ecru/off-white
822			Beige Gray - LT
644			Beige Gray - MED
642			Beige Gray - DK
640			Beige Gray - VY DK
3866			Mocha Brown - ULT VY LT
3033			Mocha Brown - VY LT
3782			Mocha Brown - LT
3032			Mocha Brown - MED
3024			Brown Gray - VY LT
3023			Brown Gray - LT
3022			Brown Gray - MED
3787			Brown Gray - DK
3021			Brown Gray - VY DK
3072			Beaver Gray - VY LT
648			Beaver Gray - LT
647			Beaver Gray - MED
646			Beaver Gray - DK
645			Beaver Gray - VY DK
535			Ash Gray - VY LT
844			Beaver Gray - ULT DK
762			Pearl Gray - VY LT
415			Pearl Gray
318			Steel Gray - LT
414			Steel Gray - DK
317			Pewter Gray
413			Pewter Gray - DK
3799			Pewter Gray - VY DK
310			Black

PICASSO Chart

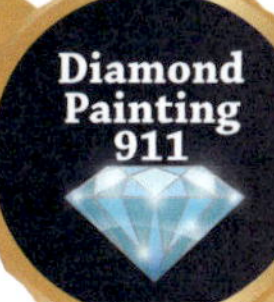

DMC	Color	Drill	DMC	Color	Drill	DMC	Color	Drill	DMC	Color	Drill	DMC	Color	Drill	DMC	Color	Drill
3713			3805			157			367			783			3859		
761			3804			159			319			782			3858		
760			151			160			890			781			3857		
3712			605			161			989			780			3774		
3328			604			996			988			746			950		
347			603			3843			987			676			3771		
353			602			995			986			729			3773		
352			601			3846			772			680			3064		
351			150			3845			3348			3829			407		
350			600			3844			3347			3822			3772		
349			3609			3761			3346			3821			632		
817			3608			519			3345			3820			3743		
3708			3607			518			895			3852			453		
3706			718			3760			704			445			452		
3705			917			517			703			307			451		
3801			915			3842			702			444			3861		
666			554			162			701			3078			3860		
321			553			747			700			727			712		
777			552			3765			699			726			739		
304			550			3766			907			725			738		
498			153			807			906			3823			437		
816			211			806			905			745			436		
815			210			3811			904			744			435		
814			209			598			472			743			868		
894			208			597			471			728			434		
893			3837			3810			470			742			433		
892			327			3809			469			741			801		
891			3747			3808			937			740			898		
957			341			3849			936			973			938		
956			156			3848			935			972			3371		
963			155			3847			934			971			543		
3716			340			964			3053			970			3864		
962			3746			959			3052			947			3863		
961			333			958			3051			946			3862		
3833			794			3812			524			900			842		
3832			793			3851			523			608			841		
3831			792			913			522			606			840		
819			791			3850			520			3824			839		
818			158			993			3364			3341			779		
776			803			992			3363			3340			838		
3326			3807			3814			3362			3825			3790		
899			3840			991			165			722			3781		
335			3839			564			3819			721			3031		
309			3838			563			166			720			White		
326			800			562			581			922			B5200		
3354			809			561			580			921			Blanc		
152			799			3817			734			920			3865		
3733			798			3816			733			919			Ecru		
3731			797			3815			732			918			822		
3350			790			504			731			3770			644		
3689			820			3813			730			951			642		
3688			828			503			3013			945			640		
3687			827			502			3012			3856			3866		
3803			813			501			3011			402			3033		
3685			826			500			372			3776			3782		
225			825			928			371			301			3032		
224			824			927			370			400			3024		
223			3756			168			834			300			3023		
3722			775			169			833			3855			3022		
3721			3841			926			832			3854			3787		
221			3325			3768			831			3853			3021		
770			3755			924			107			3827			3072		
3727			794			955			030			977			648		
316			322			954			829			976			647		
3726			312			913			613			3826			646		
315			311			912			612			975			645		
3802			336			911			611			948			535		
902			823			910			610			754			844		
3042			939			909			3047			758			762		
3041			505			3818			3046			3778			415		
3740			3753			163			3045			356			318		
154			3752			164			677			3830			414		
3836			932			966			422			355			317		
3835			931			369			3828			3777			413		
3834			930			368			869			967			3799		
3806			3750			320			420			3779			310		

Made in the USA
Monee, IL
07 July 2026

56548197R00019